ONE HOUR BEFORE THE DAWN

ONE HOUR BEFORE THE DAWN

Rod Walford

Iriswhite Publishing
Where the heart is

One Hour Before the Dawn

Iriswhite Publishing
Where the heart is

For information, visit
www.iriswhite.com

ISBN: 0-971-10721-1

Printed in the United States of America

DEDICATION

I have seen majesty in the rising of the sun
And dominion in her abdication.
I have seen supremacy in the stars
And heard authority on the rolling gale.
In the roar of the ocean, and in her lullaby,
There is both inspiration and solace.
This is to exist.

I have seen sincerity in your companionship;
Truth and forgiveness in your eyes.
I have felt warmth in the touch of your hand
And contentment of soul.
There is happiness in your proximity
And none without.
This is to live.

This book is dedicated to the woman I love.

Rod Walford

CONTENTS

Man's Best Friend

In Time

Humour

Faith

Conflict

Love

APPRECIATIONS

To friends, fellow poets and correspondents who have, in various ways, supported and inspired me in my efforts, I express my heartfelt gratitude and appreciation.

FROM NEW ZEALAND

Emanuel Seafont

A selfless campaigner and great believer in justice. A prolific writer and poet, Emanuel is legendary for his tireless efforts on behalf of his fellows. His graphic poem "In an Asian River" was the inspiration for my poem "The Flag." I am grateful to him for providing me with background information, and proud to be associated with Emanuel by way of our poem "The Final Call" which we co-authored in 1999.

Rhonda Bartle

Winner of last year's Katherine Mansfield Short Story award, Rhonda has been very supportive of my poetry. She has a charismatic sense of humor. It is most gratifying to receive feedback from such a talented author. I am always grateful for her critique of my work.

Gabrielle Burt

A gifted poet. The first message I ever received on the New Zealand Writers' Website message board was from Gabrielle, with compliments on my poem "Ben." We have stayed in touch ever since, and I am privileged to have met her in person. Our writing styles are similar, which led to a mutual understanding of each others' work. We hope to produce a co-written poem in the fullness of time.

Ann Pascoe

A well-known New Zealand musician who set the words of my poems "Reflections of your Heart" and "One Hour Before the Dawn" to music. I had the privilege of meeting Ann in person last year and was highly impressed with her professional approach. She has become one of my closest friends.

Joseph Fone

A poet whom I can only describe as magnificent. His poetry is grand and sweeping; an absolute delight to read. His classic style is timeless, and brilliantly portrayed.

John Clinton Pirtle

A relative newcomer to the New Zealand poetry scene. I have been privileged to preview some of his work, and predict he will go far. His vision spans a wide spectrum, and he has the ability to produce poetry over a wide range of subject matter.

Trish Fong

Such a beautiful poet. Her work is brilliantly descriptive and begs the reader to scan the lines over and over. Such is the power of the visual artistry which she conjures up.

James George

James has been a constant inspiration to me for years, through the medium of the New Zealand Writers' weekly chat and message board. His wit and repartee are razor sharp, and carry the hallmark of wisdom. I am thrilled for him that he has achieved long-deserved recognition with the publication of his book "Wooden Horses." I strongly recommend this superb work.

Papakura East Presbyterian Church Creative Writers' Group members

Particularly Margaret Poletti, Tani Witter and Kathy Seccombe. Each of these talented ladies has been of invaluable assistance to me. A very special thank-you to Kathy and her husband, Geoff, for the wonderful help and support they gave me during my recent difficult times. They have become the best friends I ever had. Kathy is capable of producing the most beautiful Christian poetry, and is also a gifted singer.

FROM THE UNITED STATES

Leon and Sondra Schlossberg

Owners and editors of the "Webstatic" poetry site. This father and daughter team accorded me the great honor of selecting me as one of their "showcase" poets. They have been very complimentary and supportive, and played a major role in honing my awareness of the Internet as a vehicle for sharing poetry. I will always be most grateful to them for their support and encouragement.

Betty Brown

From South Carolina. I first "met" Betty when we posted our poetry on the VP website. Betty has a talent for writing poetry that mirrors her feelings for her friends and family, and her role as a mother. She is a gifted singer and has performed publicly on many occasions. I am very grateful to her for her kind appraisals and for continuing to provide encouragement, even throughout my long periods of Internet silence.

Deb Engelke

A fellow contributor to the New Zealand Writers' poetry site, Deb has an ability to write straight from the heart. Her work is touching and easy to relate to. She is an outstanding poet who has been very kind and generous in her appreciation of my own work. I have known her for years. We have helped each other through our darkest hours and personal tragedies. One day soon we are going to be married.

ONE HOUR BEFORE THE DAWN

IN TRIBUTE

One Hour Before The Dawn

She stands alone, small, cold and frail,
A light rain falls on the Cenotaph's rail
On a cold and bleak foreboding morn,
At just one hour before the dawn.

She feels no pain, she sheds no tears,
Her thoughts transcending through the years;
Her noble head is bowed in prayer,
Stilled in the time she lost him there . . .

On a lonely field in a place called hell,
Of battle flame and raining shell,
His injured comrade on his back,
He carried through his grim attack.

Yet fate was cruel – the sniper's round
That cut her husband to the ground
Served only as a bridge in time
Beyond it's unforgiving line . . .

She may not walk, ere years must pass
But still remains his faithful lass;
No other man his place could take
Nor share her picnic by the lake.

And now on each remembrance morn,
At just one hour before the dawn;
The hallowed hour at which he fell,
His spirit moves, in her to dwell.

As dark horizon turns to grey,
The pipes lament the break of day;
The wreaths of poppies laid with love
Pay homage to the souls above.

She lifts her head now, dignified;
And in her eyes, the glow of pride
For, tightly held in her dear hand
The one that wears his wedding band . . .

She holds the secret so long cherished
The symbol of a love unperished
And in the dawn light's ghostly pallor
The simple wording reads "For Valour."

Bereavement's shadow drapes its cloak
Around the widow's heart of oak
Behold! – the weight of tragic loss
She bears as One who bore the Cross.

Unknown, uncounted days remain
Then she'll be with her love again.
In Heaven's mirror, brightly viewed,
Her country's love – and gratitude.

Lest we forget to bear in mind
The ladies who were left behind,
Though age may weary and condemn,
We ever should remember them.

Their courage knows no bounds of time,
Though earthly flesh may wither;
Whoever would true valour see
Let him come hither.

A Stable Friendship

How soon the summer leaves have cooled and changed to amber gold!
And with the season's turn, my mind revisits times of old.
Sweet morning mists, warm summer days and eventide's soft bliss,
With crowning golden sunsets – England's summer evening kiss.

'Twas in that sleepy Sussex village, by the Rother's tranquil course,
Where first we met, we keepers of the garden and the horse;
Where smoothest flank and quarters hind that found my eyes returning
Were not that born of equine form, nor of a fleeting yearning.

Oh No! 'twas something finer still, – a mystical attraction,
I longed that you would feel it too, that spark . . . that hot reaction.
Damn the conscience which prohibits what a married man could say
To a jodhpur wearing princess when she's feeding horses hay.

What magic in those honeyed curls, where sunbeam's playful dancing
Would frame your pastel eyes and lips – bewitching, all-entrancing!
Such jewels there would dance, like silver salmon in a stream;
So that just to stand beside you was a living, breathing dream.

Your speech so eloquent, refined, – its strange hypnotic power
Would ever linger in my mind – caress each passing hour.
Your very nearness spurred my pulse to race, and heart to hammer,
As such charisma and panache would any man enamour!

There was just a hint of perfume – it was Lentheric's "mystique"
As it mingled with the saddle soap, thus would my ardour peak.
'Midst the hay and straw and barley, and the bridles in a row,
Precious moments in your presence were the best I'd come to know.

How well we laughed and chatted in that little tack room stall
Where we had our tea and biscuits as we watched the snowflakes fall.
While your heart was light and happy then, my own was close to breaking,
As the horses munched their haynets, of their daily feed partaking;

On the day I found my courage, and I told you how I felt,
You confessed there was another, and I felt my spirit melt.
But he had a guilty secret, he betrayed a woman's trust
Just like me, he was a victim of the war 'twixt love and lust.

Yet I saw beyond your fragile pose, and feelings that controlled me;
The mirrors of your soul belied the words which your lips told me.
Vibrations from your heart were stronger than your spoken word,
Which made our farewell . . . madness! . . . to the point of the absurd.

Though the voice of reason begged me, I had banned it from my ears,
So all-consuming was the beauty of your five and twenty years;
But your wisdom, it was stronger, and it touched me to the core;
While the lust went undefeated, it was love that won the war.

So, for you I wrote "The Eagle" – at the time I didn't know it,
That a decade down the line, they would consider me a poet.
Yes, our parting was sweet sorrow, you were tender, you were fine,
Though I have no part of your life . . . you're forever part of mine.

THE AUTHOR

He portrays a lonely figure
In his cottage by the sea
With his pencil and his paper and his dog.
Gone his youthful verve and vigour
But remaining in its lee
Is the gift that soon will form his epilogue.

With the ocean panorama
Bathed in twilight's amber glow,
He reflects upon his cherished thoughts and dreams.
Playing out a lifetime's drama.
As his passions ebb and flow,
High above, a solitary seagull screams.

Though his clothes may hang in tatters
And his hair be long and grey
Yet his eyes still sparkle brightly as he writes.
For in literary matters
He is half a world away
And upon his works will thousands set their sights.

They will never know the sorrow,
They will never know the pain
That has forged the man behind the flowing pen.
Yet adversity's tomorrow
Brings a refuge from the rain
Where his reader may find shelter . . . now and then.

Once a student, once a teacher,
Once a lover, once a friend,
The seed now feeds the hand that once did sow it.
A philanthropist, a preacher,
Altruistic to the end
He's theorist, philosopher . . . and poet.

He's the universal writer,
He's the champion of choice;
Every corner of each foreign field he calls.
He's the independent fighter,
He's the literary voice;
He will touch your heart before the sunset falls.

DEEP REGRETS

The protocols of men of power;
Agendas passed in hiding.
Procrastination steals the hour,
Now there is none abiding.

Unseen, forsaken in the deep.
Paralysis sub-zero.
A frozen slumber's tragic keep.
The silence of the hero.

As nations feel all hope recede,
One hundred men and more
Lay perished now, through lack of heed
Upon the ocean floor.

Entombed in freezing Arctic flows,
Their deeds for evermore
Recalled in ice-bound echoes
Where the elements do war.

O Trinity of love and power,
Receive into thy grace
These men, who in their final hour
The cruel seas embrace.

Let every man who evermore
'Neath lonely sea or sky
Shall sail, remember, – there but for
The grace of God go I.

*Dedicated to the memory of the 118 men
of the Russian submarine "Kursk" which exploded
and sank in the Barents Sea, August 12, 2000.*

THE AMERICA'S CUP

Borne forth in grandest splendour on Hauraki's fickle breezes
One point to port brings halyards taut – the swirling dervish teases;
Fine honed bows scythe through foaming crests, perchance to win the day,
As one by one, the dreams of nations slowly ebb away.
The faith of Aotearoa guides one tried and steadfast keel
As sixteen men who work their Magic whet their nerves of steel;
To give their all, as we enthrall, and crystal waters smile
Upon the fortunes of the brave and father Beaufort's guile
In search of dreams through plotted schemes of yachting's greatest prize,
Must give no quarter, doubt nor falter – Red Moon's on the rise!
The watching world shall see unfurled the strength of Neptune's sons
Whose Kiwi way will seize the day and spike Italian guns.
Return again, Francesco! for the Black Boat, still, she lies
Her masthead broom, a clean swept room, it sweetly signifies.

MUSICAL MEMORIES

Discernment, like a wine, matures as years go rolling by,
Reflected in the mirror of the music that we buy.
But ever we remember that which echoed in our youth
Those favourite songs we oft recall, of life and love and truth.

Do the memories come flooding when you hear a Beach Boys number?
Can the golden voice of Jim Reeves stir those past thoughts
    from their slumber?
Does the memory of Roy Orbison still linger on your mind?
Yet the lyrics of Bob Dylan never leave the past behind?

Did you ever dance the night away to Rod's dramatic tones?
Or take a friend to see a concert by the Rolling Stones?
And back in '74, did your appreciation heighten
When Abba first sang "Waterloo" upon the stage in Brighton?

But now that time has washed us down its ever rolling stream,
And re-defined our preference a little more serene;
Despite nostalgia's journey, which we take in mood reflective,
The chances are our current trends are somewhat more selective.

Does the voice of Pavarotti with your inner spirit mingle?
At the close of "Nessun Dorma" does your spine begin to tingle?
Do you empathise with Elton, and his "Candle" for Diana?
Or can "Someone Saved My Life Tonight" evoke you in like manner?

Do the pipes of Scotland stir you, reaching deep down in your soul?
Or the strings of Mantovani, or the voice of Nat "King" Cole?
What of lovely Sarah Brightman, with her pitch so crystal clear,
Harmonising (with Bocelli) at the peak of her career?

Have you listened to the moving "Words"? – If you're a Bee Gees fan
Then you'll thrill to Robin's haunting anthem of the Isle of Man.
When the summer day is over, and its busy cares have flown,
Just relax with John McDermott, and you'll never feel alone.

There can be few among us, be we husbands, be we wives,
Who stand untouched, in whole or part, by music in our lives.
In truth, it is the food of love and keeps the spirit younger;
Play on, musicians! – feed us well, that none shall ever hunger.

THUNDER IN THE AIR

The die is cast . . . exhaust pipes blast a deafening fanfare;
There is tension in the atmosphere . . . and thunder in the air.
Malaysia's white-hot cauldron turns a furnace of raw power
As its fever grips the faithful that awaited on the hour.

You could feel the ground reverberate beneath the trumpet blast . . .
Any second now the lights will change the future to the past.
And each driver in his cockpit feels it jarring through his knees . . .
As the heat inside his nomex reaches fifty-odd degrees.

It was all-on in a moment, in a blinding flash of time
As the decibel responded to the tacho needle's climb;
Screaming rubber scorched the tarmac, in a frantic bid for traction
Launching men, machines and Murray into vibrant full-on action.

Sound vibrations hit the ether from the mighty engines' roar
Forty thousand unleashed horsepower, blasting down the straight
         . . . full bore.
In a test of nerve and sinew, and the power of the beast . . .
Let the devil take the hindmost . . . who shall touch his brakes the least?

There are two Ferraris foremost, with McLaren close behind
There's a Honda belching smoke and fire . . . and Arrows flying blind;
There are Jordans, Jags and Williams, and they're fighting for their lives
On their pit mechanics shoulders, rests who fails . . . and who survives.

Then, a sudden expectation fell upon the thronging crowds
As a change of fortune threatened in the dark, foreboding clouds.
Now the mighty legions gamble for a second's worth of gain
Lies defeated in the slipstream of a pace-car in the rain.

There is contact on the airwaves, there is frenzy in the pits
There is victory in the offing for the man who keeps his wits.
It's a testing game of patience, but the track begins to dry
Now the prancing horse is dancing 'neath the lightening of the sky.

It's a duel of mortal combat as the throttles open wide
They are screaming from the pitlane in an angry roaring tide.
They are laying down the power, fifteen thousand revs and more
There is valour in the heartbeat, there is sweat in every pore.

Here is Michael on the rampage . . . in his eyes, a glint of steel;
There's McLaren close behind him, with the Scot behind the wheel;
There's a flying Dutchman driving as he's never done before
And a Finn who's pulling all the stops to even up the score.

It's a battle of endurance in the ever rising heat,
But those scything red Ferraris never seem to miss a beat.
Not a sign of overheating, nor a faint ignition lag
It's a one-two high-speed convoy right up to the chequered flag.

There was justice in the victory . . . it was true, and well deserved
By the men who wore the laurels, and by those who also served.
And the gallant Scotsman, he was there . . . a third upon the day;
But shall surely rise . . . no compromise . . . for that's McLaren's way.

From an idea by Geoff Seccombe.
Based on the Malaysian Grand Prix 2001.

REFLECTION

TIMELESS

Today I stood upon the shore
Where Grandad walked in days of yore;
Along its sandy, glossy sheen
Where once, his imprint would have been.

And thereupon I did behold
'Twas here, when I was two years old;
I dangled from his stalwart hands
In gleeful awe of foaming sands.

So timeless now, this scene appears
It's altered not these fifty years
Nor hundreds, thousands gone before;
As restless wave greets silent shore.

Still endless rolling surf she brings;
Now to my little son she sings.
I held him in her gentle lee,
The way my Grandad once held me.

As every wavelet's dying throes
Washed tiny grains between my toes;
Methought perhaps, that in his day,
For every grain, a pebble lay.

– Timeless –

Eroded by the tick and tock
Of oscillating tidal clock;
Its pulsing rhythm, all abounding
In softest kiss, or anger pounding.

I pondered what it all may mean;
Our ocean's mighty time machine.
Where pebbles, hardened, flat or round,
By rolling surf to sand are ground.

From rock to stone to pebbled grain
To sand, and back to rock again . . .
As, in our turn, we surely must
Become as ashes . . . dust to dust.

ICE CASTLES IN THE SKY

Oh! you elected minions, who in your towers of ivory repose
Insulated by cocoons woven from broken threads of promised intent;
Twisting words with eloquence to suit your purpose
As it bends and sways in the fickle draught of self-indulgence.

You dwell among the ramparts of power and control
Treading the dark corridors of deception and trickery;
Behind the iron-barred portcullis of the fortress of bureaucracy
Where well meaning hearts, fast hardened in the dollar's
     white-hot forge
Become as tempered steel – a sword to strike at freedom's
     hard won shield.
What misguided force is it that seeks to govern the human spirit?
Never will it surrender to the intrusive microchip, nor become slave
     to oppressive dictates.

Freedom? She will ride high in her victory, as sure as there is only
     one true flight.
As the arrow, straight from the bow flies, so the words
     from the hearts of the just shall penetrate the transparent walls
     of your ice castles in the sky.
Your crystalline fragments shall fall, shattered in ignominy,
And the root of all evil be exposed for its true worth.

Ah! That you and I are one in spirit.
Fellow poets, and seekers of the truth, that we may see the secrets
     of the impostor, and thus protect our world of shared beauty.
Let us rejoice in our unity, and be secure in empathy, yes,
     and stronger still.
That we may know our spirit will be carried to a place far beyond
     the melting remnants of the ice castles in the sky.

DECEPTION

Deception, like a viper, lurks
'Neath every stone of human works;
In all the fields of our endeavour
Lies his agenda . . . subtle . . . clever.

His motive, as a virus, spreads
And infiltrates ambitious heads;
Corruption's spectrum knows no bounds,
No refuge from its baying hounds.

Scheming, plotting, cunning minds
Devising minefields of all kinds
That honest man and learned scholar
Be parted from their hard-won dollar.

And who has not yet felt his bite?
His plans are laid both day and night;
He knows no shame, nor feels remorse
When through your veins, hot blood shall course!

Short lived, the serpent's profit gained,
His hands shall be forever stained;
Yet ne'er will reconcile his goal
To gain the world . . . he sold his soul.

THE MIRROR

Let us take a glass of wine, by this fireside of mine,
Let us dwell on truths and tragedies, my friend.
We shall delve into our soul, by the warmly glowing coal;
We shall question, yet we may not comprehend.

Flicker, little fiery tongues! – as kismet's fickle fingers
Play concertos on the heartstrings of our years.
Ah! we may be certain that the harshest lesson lingers,
Though foreboding tolled her warning in our ears.

Have we not spent far too long, on contentious right and wrong?
Have we not been overburdened by our trial?
Have we not aspired to cease, to embrace an inner peace?
Have we craved no hushed respite . . . for just a while?

In this mirage of enigmas, from the moment of our birth
We have chased elusive shadows on a wall.
We have heard the boastful discourse as the pompous flaunt their worth,
And lamented dying echoes as they fall.

We are kindred of the humble man, our empathy is stark;
And his quiet, softly spoken word is kind.
Let his unassuming courage be our beacon in the dark
And his ethic be as succour to our mind.

Now I look into your eyes, as the firelight slowly dies,
And I realize that onward we must go.
Unended is the battle, and it brooks no compromise,
For tomorrow we must face the unknown foe.

You're the silent one I've known through the years as they have flown;
You're the friend to whom I cannot tell a lie.
For the mirror on the wall holds the form who tells me all . . .
And the soul whose truth I surely can't deny.

SANDS OF MY HEART

The autumn turns to winter and the leaves blow through the door
The seagull turns her icy glance along an empty shore.
The beach is all deserted now, the ocean cold and bleak
Its blues and hues have turned to grey, all muted, quiet and weak.

Now more than thirty years have passed since last I saw your face.
I wonder if you're near, or if, in some far distant place
You ever sit and reminisce, in quiet thoughtful pose;
And ponder all your memories as you trace the path you chose.

Do you gaze downward from the bridge, where time's fast waters flow,
Along the pathways of your life . . . how fast your children grow!
And do you spare a passing thought for absent friends you knew
In far-off days . . . in summer haze . . . when cares were far and few?

When spring turns into summertime, blue skies return once more
And laughing children build their castles on the sandy shore.
Though sun-kissed lovers surf the waves, with love-light in their eyes;
The test of time will surely find regret in long-lost ties.

For friendship's hand is precious, and its hold will life enhance
I wish I'd held yours tighter, when you first gave me the chance;
And yet somehow, I look back now, and though we're far apart
You're still there . . . right beside me . . . on the warm sands of my heart.

BRIXHAM 1966

Rekindled, visions of my childhood's day
Do visit me in thoughts of old Torbay.
Oh Glorious Devon! How your red heart bleeds
In all your scattered offsprings' worldly deeds.

How well that little fishing village nestles;
Whose quaysides teem with art and chugging vessels.
The night's red sky, the cloth capped skippers wish;
When Brixham's trawlers taught the world to fish.

All Saints' presides, an ageless, stony aunt,
Where little streets of Furzeham slope and slant.
That beckoned Orange William once to stand;
Where still he reigns, in concrete, on The Strand.

Distress flares bark their thunder from beyond,
And brave hearts in the dead of night respond
To waken Princess Alex from her sleep;
Alert, her crew their constant vigil keep.

Torbay, your glow of evening's amber light
Inspired Henry Frances in God's sight.
On Berry Head, across your golden sea
He wrote his mighty hymn . . . "Abide With Me."

Where, years later, as a boy I'd roam
From Brixham's famous "Sons of Sailors" Home.
Perchance, I tarried there, on that same spot;
Becoming what I am . . . and what I'm not.

Now, through a darkened glass, I see the world,
Yet Devon's where my childhood banner's furled.
Where breaking waters foam, and mackerel play
As gently sets the sun on old Torbay.

BITTER HARVEST

I have savoured many wines from a hundred different vines
On the hillsides where temptation's fruits are crammed.
Where the all-enticing finger of beelzebub does linger
Bidding welcome . . . to the valley of the damned.

Oh! how sweet the mocker's lure, 'tis a goodly thing and pure
To my blinkered eyes of innocence she calls.
Come, your lustful passions slake, of my wanton fruits partake
Let your secrets stay cocooned within these walls.

Now, in anguish I am smothered, for a wine I have discovered
That is honey-sweet as nectar to my soul.
And the glass which holds it true has so rare a crystal hue
That it's light could weld my heart, and make it whole.

If I'd only known of old what the prophets had foretold
That where're a man may roam, his sins shall follow.
For there is no hiding place from the great Creator's face
He can reach the smallest cleft . . . or darkest hollow.

But, alas, I must depart with this grieving, broken heart
For experience, she keeps so dear a school.
Yes, I tell you true, my friend, and remember to the end
For she loves no better scholar than a fool!

"Experience keeps a dear school – and a fool
will learn in no other."

THE PROSTITUTE

His smile is warm, his lips sincere,
His kiss upon her cheek
Brings memories of yesteryear,
Before her limbs grew weak.

In those good times, she was able,
Now she sees him to the door
In her wheelchair, by the table
On their polished hallway floor.

His purpose is not hidden
From her sharp, perceptive mind.
Her thoughts, by reason, bidden
Are the understanding kind.

Their love is deep and timeless
Yet she knows his carnal plight;
And prays for God's forgiveness
When his sin is done this night.

On flagstones cold and dim-lit,
As his footsteps gather pace;
Gut churning, like a gimlet
Comes the lure of scent and lace.

He knows the risk he's taking,
And perchance he'll burn in hell.
Now his trembling hand is shaking
But his finger finds the bell.

Her smile is feigned and formal
And her bosom full and wide.
Her air is calm and normal,
And she beckons him inside.

He hangs his coat upon the hook,
His trousers on the chair.
She slips her gown, that he may look
Upon her body bare.

Her breasts are firm and striking
And her shapely thighs are good.
Between them, to his liking
Rests her badge of womanhood.

She comes to him with open arms
His blood begins to race.
He fondles her seductive charms,
And tender fingers trace . . .

They lay down gently, passion burns,
And as she takes him there,
He shuts his eyes, as time returns . . .
And gone, her wheelchair.

He calls her name with passion
At the moment of his peak.
Then she answers in like fashion;
Poignant words which leave him weak.

They lay an hour, he tells her much,
Then reaches for his purse.
She stalls his hand with gentle touch,
Her manner like a nurse.

As home-help she had often
Pushed that wheelchair to the store.
And honeyed eyes would soften;
Lonely ladies both, that's sure.

Now she will not take his money
For her heart is moved indeed.
And she knows a mere "bye, honey"
Cannot gratify his need.

She closed the door, he looked around,
And paused as he reflected;
As kind a heart as e'er he'd found
Beat where he least expected.

Her sins may be as scarlet,
Still yet chances by and by
The teardrop of a harlot . . .
From a seldom moistened eye.

TRUST

Eye-to-eye conveyed, and in soft whispers
    of the evening brings delight
To friends and lovers soaring on the wings
    of love's true flight.
Yet must the heart be wary should the shadow
    of betrayal once alight
That turns the warmth of summer to the frozen heart
    of winter's night.

For what is trust? Intangible, yet by truth and deed alone
    she must be earned
By spirit born, and sought by every heart which for love
    has ever yearned.
There is no soul more deeply pierced, nor by
    the fires of hell severely burned
Than that which gives its one true love completely,
    but had contempt returned.

Summer In Brighton & Hove (1966)

Time was, as I fond remember
I, from June until September
Spent my adolescent years
By the famous Brighton piers.

Promenades and esplanades.
Picnic baskets, bright sunshades.
Kiddies Punch and Judy shows.
Little beach huts all in rows.

Suntanned bodies strewn around.
Blankets on the beach and ground.
Candy floss and ice-cream cones.
Children playing on the stones.

Sallies on the bandstand play
Timeless airs of yesterday.
Tourists to the Palace flock
For a stick of Brighton rock.

See the gloss of new-born sand
As the tide withdraws its hand.
Wave crests sparkle in the sun.
Helter-skelter rides are fun.

– SummerIn Brighton & Hove (1966) –

Speedboat rides between the piers.
Lemonades and ginger beers.
Long parades of grand hotels
Hear the ghost-train's ringing bells.

Peter Pan is still alive
By the wide Madeira Drive.
There's a little railway track
Takes you there – and brings you back.

Now, when I lay my head to rest,
And think of things I love the best;
There's one of which I e'er shall boast . . .
My memoirs of the Sussex coast.

White Knight – Black Knight

When I was a young boy, I once had a book;
Through bright coloured pages and pictures I'd look.
There were white knights and black knights and kings and princesses
And ladies at court in their long flowing dresses.

There were vagabonds mingled with merchants and traders,
And castles assaulted by hooded invaders.
With ramparts and moats that encircled great walls,
And boys stealing apples from market place stalls.

That the white knights were good, and the black knights were bad
Was the total extent of the knowledge I had.
In each duel they fought, I was thrilled to the core;
For the fate of the black knight was certain and sure.

What a wonderful feeling to think, if I stood
On the side of the bold and the true and the good
And swore my allegiance to country and king,
I'd be safe from the threat any black knight could bring.

Now the years have passed on, and my rose coloured vision
Is blurred and obscured by the sword of division.
So through a glass darkly, and try as I may,
I see all the knights in a dim shade of grey.

I still see the vagabonds, traders and thieves,
(Though often the difference eludes and deceives.)
Whilst kings and princesses still hide behind walls
Now hooded invaders transpose to house calls.

But all who have fought and all who have died
With banners of courage and truth at their side,
Have seen in past glories their stories predicted
As scenes from my childhood pictures depicted.

The bright shield of honour upholds its ideals
And gallantry spawns on its moral appeals.
Have you not heard his voice in the depths of your heart?
The white knight of valour . . . he still plays his part.

THE HEART OF WINTER

Spring is for the spirit that is young and wild and free,
Summer is the time for being all you want to be.
Autumn is a moment for reflecting on the past;
To gather strength in readiness for winter's icy blast.

So easy is the living when the sun is warm and bright,
And vivid is its contrast with the chill of winter's night.
When summer evenings turn into the frosty white of dawn,
And you walk the hard road, haunted by wicked winter's scorn . . .

Remember whence your courage and your character were found . . .
'Twas surely not in Autumn's gold, nor springtime's fertile ground.
Nor summer's blissful soft embrace, sweet as her kiss may be,
Oh no! it was another steeped in cold adversity.

Like an iceberg in the ocean, you have hidden strengths below,
That were formed in life's cold waters from your tears of melting snow.
So the heart that beats within you, as it pulses, like a star
Takes its strength from your life's winters
    . . . they have made you what you are.

MAN'S BEST
FRIEND

BEN

In sheepdog trials, your father won, whilst mother worked the sheep;
Together they have gifted you with assets buried deep,
A handsome face, intelligence, agility and speed,
With heart so true and loyal, such a credit to your breed.

Your paw-pads crunching softly on the icy grass
The frost-hung beech hedge in the moonlight basks
The silver light of moon deflecting
Dances in your eyes, reflecting.

Such faith in lovely eyes, which, like bright amber, shine
As the coal-black sheen of your coat at brushing time.
Ah! how your handsome features mirror images of night!
With your cloak of darkest charcoal, and your blaze of snowy white.

Yet, what is it that endears you so, that quality so treasured?
That great unspoken attribute, alas, so oft unmeasured,
But loyalty, the priceless gift revered above all other
Which neither time can render mute nor earthly distance smother.

In summer's careful warmth, 'midst June's orchestral sound
We walked and ran together, field and woodland all around,
In pedigree you stand as one of England's finest breed
Empowered by the instinct so exemplified by deed.

– Ben –

As golden crown of setting sun dropped slowly from the skies
You would sit and tell me stories with your telepathic eyes
No words were ever needed, and none were ever said,
But you always got the message through before you went to bed!

Now destiny and circumstance, those pruning tools of time,
Combined to part us sooner than did any plans of mine;
I grieve that we were miles apart when you were laid to rest
But in my heart you'll always be just what you were – the best!

As Omar once reminded us, the moving finger writes,
And I look back on our friendship over countless days and nights
It is my hope, it is my prayer, the day we meet again,
We'll run in those Eternal fields, my faithful, dear old Ben.

A tribute to my Border Collie.

STORM

Dark clouds in sombre brooding rolled
The seas to darkest grey,
As in the hermit's croft, a cold
Chill stole the light away.

Old Jim knelt by the fireside close
And stroked the fur so warm;
He looked beyond the old black nose
Into the eyes of Storm.

And what he saw there took him back
Some fifteen years before,
When elements combined to wrack
His Scottish island shore . . .

The gale in squalling anger thrashed,
Black thunderclouds were spoiling.
Cruel rain in glassy needles lashed
The sea to cauldron boiling.

Wild lightning set the skies afire,
Harsh thunder clamoured scorn;
Such tempest did all hell conspire!
The night the pup was born.

Old Jim, by lamp of kerosene,
In meagre shed presided
Upon a birth which might have been
By Providence provided.

Twas at the tumult's raging height
Beyond the 'witching hour
Those first drawn breaths in dead of night
Defied the thunder's power.

– Storm –

And in the cold, soft, eerie light
That was the grey dawn's form,
In memory of that fearful night
He named his new pup . . . Storm.

'Twixt man and Border Collie grew
Such bond of faith unspoken
Which through the years was born anew
And still remains unbroken.

Oft in routine where doubt would lie,
Approval would prevail
By telepathic amber eye,
Or wag of bushy tail.

So in that sparse, unyielding land
Bereft of nature's frills;
Storm learned survival's sleight of hand
And honed his shepherd skills.

As when that mighty taloned, beaked
Assassin of the skies
In predatory plummet peaked,
None heard the young lamb's cries . . .

Save Storm, who from his watch-post raced
With speed of bullet rifled.
Not since, that hawk, by jaws embraced
With lamb nor flock had trifled!

Old Jim recalled the moment well,
When fishing was his love;
He sore misjudged the ocean swell
'Spite barking from above . . .

The towering wave that plucked him
From his rugged rocky pier,
His vision rendered vaguely dim;
The hand of death was near . . .

In depths of frenzied tidal rip
On jagged rocks he smote,
Then felt the jaws of courage grip
The collar of his coat.

Storm pulled with all his strength and might
In mortal combat matched;
'Til from the crazed foam's deadly bite
His master's life he snatched.

Thus many halcyon years passed
In work and play and slumber
But fate's cold hand in dice-play cast
One final deadly number.

Old Jim grew weaker, pale and gaunt
He knew his time was brief.
And radiation scarce would daunt
This creeping tissue thief.

Time's rolling stream flowed, unrestrained.
Yet Storm, he knew the score;
As Father Time, alas, constrained
His legs, once swift and sure.

Now, in the embers' dying glow
Jim raised his trembling hand,
And softly stroked the face that so
Much seemed to understand.

Then, as he closed his eyes in prayer,
And life began to end,
Upon his cheek, a last kiss there
Came from his dearest friend.

Outside, the moon, in mourning bowed,
Her silver gleam in hiding
As once again, the thunder growled
In dark, foreboding tiding.

As Storm lay down beside Old Jim
The air grew damp and colder.
He rested weary head and limb
Upon the old man's shoulder.

And as the rain began to fall
Upon that lowly croft
Storm heard his master's final call
Ride on the gale aloft.

So well he knew that nature's power,
The herald of his birth,
Bore tribute to the very hour
He'd end his time on earth.

On midnight's breath of rolling gale
Two spirits rose as one
No bond of love can time assail
. . . In Heaven's morning sun.

SAMSON

They called him Samson, but in jest.
They knew he wouldn't be the best.
The last of six, the little runt,
He'd never make it to the front.

And thus he grew, upon the farm,
Did little good, but did no harm.
But daily he was made to scoot
By dint of master's savage boot.

Who cared but not a jot, it seemed,
If Samson yelped, or jumped, or screamed.
His favour was reserved indeed
For those first-born among the breed.

Yet Samson, though he'd been the last
Through all the years his faith held fast.
And not once did retaliate
Though gruff his master's voice would grate.

He'd eat, and sleep, and lag behind
The others, and began to find
That not one noticed – even cared
Just how his little brother fared.

Engrossed, they were, with tending flock,
And all that moved on hoof and hock.
They were the finest – every one,
Let Samson take his kicks . . . and run.

Then came one winter, bleak and hard
The snows were deep, the cold winds jarred.
The flocks were lost, their tracks were masked
So cruel the biting polar blast.

Old farmer Jack, he had no choice
And ventured forth with stick and voice.
Five collies of stout heart and breed
Just one remained . . . Jack had no need . . .

Of him, but after half an hour
A blizzard closed with awful power.
The evening, with deceptive haste
Would darkly cloak the frozen waste.

The dogs had scattered far and wide;
Old Jack had nowhere left to hide.
As driving snowflakes stung his eyes
He slipped, and fell with great surprise . . .

Then plunged into a gully deep
And landed in a tangled heap.
A broken ankle pained him sore
He tried to rise – but could no more.

Foreboding swept upon him there
For winter had him in her lair.
He knew too well a man could die
Beneath such unrelenting sky.

Soon darkness came a-closing in
The snowstorm eased from thick to thin.
A frosty moonlight lit the scene;
No tracks remained where Jack had been.

He shouted to his dogs for help
In vain – there was no bark nor yelp.
Alone and cold, in fear and stress
Jack slipped into unconsciousness.

Much later, in the dead of night,
He re-awakened, numbed with fright
As paw-pads crunching on the snow
Seemed, in his mind, to come and go.

A sudden warmth upon his cheek!
He scarce could bring himself to speak.
Then came, at last, to realize
Such love . . . in Samson's almond eyes.

"Me lad, I've done you dreadful wrong
My oath, this will be our swan song!"
Old Jack was failing fast . . . and so
Resigned to die there in the snow.

But Samson's will was strong and bold
To keep his master from the cold,
All through the wee small hours he lay
His body like a warm duvet.

– Samson –

They lay together all night long
One heartbeat weak, the other strong.
The dying man, in rueful folly
Shielded by his Border Collie.

They found them in the dawn's soft light
The rescue helicopter flight
Directed by a small black dog
Seen through the ice-cold morning fog.

"It was a close-run thing," they said
"If not for him, you would be dead."
Old Jack stirred from his still repose,
And Samson licked him on the nose.

Now, six months later, on the farm,
You may perceive (with certain charm)
Five collies sleeping in the shed
And one stretched out . . . on old Jack's bed.

JOY

I do behold
Your nose is cold.
Your sable coat has points of gold.
Your legs grow long,
Your teeth grow strong!
Your heart grows loyal, true and bold.

I do espy
The sanguine eye
Informing me you tell no lie!
No sock you stole
Nor dug that hole
You know not who, or when or why!

I do perceive
That, by your leave,
You've chewed the end of my shirtsleeve!
Look! what's this here?
Don't lick my ear!
I love you too, I do believe!

I do surmise
Your beauty lies
Within your warm appealing eyes.
What girlish guile!
Such canine wile
Brings with your love a bond that ties.

A tribute to a little stray pup found wandering in our
garden in poor health. This poem is dedicated to our vet,
Kaye Manson, of Papakura, in gratitude for her remarkable
skill and care which played such a vital role in Joy's recovery.

IN TIME

WOMAN

Time suspended . . . self reflected . . . mirror on the wall;
Within your naked form grows warm desire to bare your soul.
And as your misty eyes perchance allow your gaze to fall
Would you incline the thief of time to give back what he stole?

The symmetry – that curve of figure, one time blessed
    with youthful vigour
Now, perhaps, those hourglass contours seem less well defined;
Where nature's yearly course has clashed with life's demanding rigour
Your soul alone retains your beauty in it's timeless mind.

Ah! Sweet forest of delight, soft secret garden of creation;
Within your warm allure is formed the seed of life renewed.
But damn him straight to hell who shall abuse it with elation,
For sure the hand of vengeance counts his evil deeds accrued.

How sharp was barbed the arrow that has pierced your
    childhood's dreams;
Illusions shipwrecked on the storm-bound oceans of your life.
Oh, woman! that your love may conquer nightmare's chilling screams,
And find safe haven from betrayal's deadly knife!

How diverse – the winds of fate where chance has dealt your hand,
If beauty, poise and grace elude your outward glance;
Then count yourself no less a part of all that nature planned;
Compassion's heartfelt understanding highlights your romance.

What pen shall e'er encompass all your wishes and desires?
What man can truly comprehend the longings of your heart?
Who can know Utopia's dream that oft your mind conspires
To shield your child from evil – and its wicked poisoned dart?

Your life shall have its pain and grief and sorrow,
Wise hearts still get broken, and well-meaning fingers burned;
Surely then, your sun shall rise tomorrow
Newly borne on wings of lessons learned.

THE STAR

I was sitting by the quayside, on a rocky harbour wall
The midnight hour had come and gone, as far as I recall.
I watched a star descending in the clear, crystal night
Deep into the far horizon, like a jewel, spangled bright.

As it slowly kissed the skyline, I perceived its brightness dim
In its mellow, calm surrender to the planetary rim.
She was one of many millions that presided o'er the deep
To survey her abdication from the nightfall's starry keep . . .

'Twas a thing of stunning beauty, as I pondered on her fate
So unto her dying glory I was prompted to relate.
She had reigned in perfect dignity for her appointed span
As, in all of his achievements, is the duty of a man.

Ah! his power, glory, riches, rise as but a fleeting thing
Like the passing of the shadow from a seagull on the wing.
Then his years become as nothing, for his fragile deeds are slight
When compared with this enchantress . . . shining diamond of the night!

She will rise again tomorrow, in the firmament above
And, beneath her, men will testify their everlasting love.
And I . . . when I at last fulfill the number of my days
Shall watch her cross the skies once more, and bid her tranquil rays

To shine upon my resting place, that in its gentle lee
My soul beholds the vision of an iridescent sea.
Where the mighty ocean witnesses the astral rise and fall
Let my spirit gaze in wonder . . . from a rocky harbour wall.

LUCRATIVE?

As commodities go, you are harmless enough
Whether tendered in coin, or in crinkly stuff.
But, without you, it seems that the world will not turn,
Men consort with the devil, your favour to earn.

They will cheat and deceive, yes, and murder as well,
And for you, more than any, damned lies they will tell.
Your repose in the hand brings a gleam to the eye
Yet, because of you, many will perish and die.

On the drug scene you loiter, malicious and hard
Where your influence creeps in an evil facade.
And the contraband, stained with the taint of your breath
May bring joy, then despair . . . and a premature death.

Though taught, as a child, I must work for your favour,
Adulthood revealed a much more distinct flavour.
For those most productive, your profits are small
While you cosset with cheats and deceivers and all . . .

Those dealers financial, behind the white collar
To justify shares in the evil drug dollar
Do patronize smugly, in form parasitic
Appearing ostensibly most analytic . . .

"We will honour your custom, regardless of source,
With the privacy act there is little recourse;
You just cover your traces and we'll do the same
It's a "dog eat dog" world in this lucrative game.

– Lucrative? –

Simply get the kids hooked and we'll all become rich
Their lives are expendable – ain't that a bitch?
Too bad for their loved ones – but, oh, what the hell?
Blind eyes we will turn if you get them as well!"

Though mighty your power, and important your deed,
You're the brother of anguish and mother of greed;
Who seek only profit, but count not the cost
For the parents who grieve . . . and the children they've lost.

Yes, in drug lords and cohorts, your minions are legion;
They launder your bloodstains throughout every region
Of banking and commerce, our lives to control,
Yet will surely atone . . . in the courts of the soul.

THE ALIEN

The shadow by the huge craft cast left Presidents and Kings aghast;
Whilst spellbound ranks of U.S. might stood muted
    by the awesome sight.
The mighty hull descended low . . . to touch the golden sand below.
Light years of interstellar quest had passed before she came to rest.

The exit ramp, extended, brought five thousand trigger fingers taut;
As global populations viewed, foreboding gripped the multitude.
A solitary figure, slight, surrounded by a silver light;
Walked slowly to the ground below to face the Presidential show.

His haunting cyber-phonic tone was calm and clear – no malice shown;
Yet amplified, that all might share, his discourse carried on the air . . .
"Withhold your weapons – have no fear! We ask no confrontation here,
  But come in peace and hope, to find the voice of reason in mankind.

Established on a distant star, we have observed you from afar;
In full accord with nature's laws, our place in time is not as yours.
Our visit brings a timely warning of the dangers that are spawning;
Shades of wars 'twixt forces strong – the conflict between
    right and wrong.

For years you've sought, in distant place, solutions for
    your troubled race
That shall be found, in whole or part, embedded in each human heart.
Time is a house with many mansions, forged in fires of vast expansions;
Whose architect has shown His face – etched in the hearts
    of the human race.

Despite advancement's rapid pace, keep caution's insight in its place;
Lest lack of heed to wisdom's call should bring destruction on you all.
Seek not your visions in the deeds of evil's mercenary creeds,
For in his purse lies grave temptation, falsehood, lies and condemnation.

Hypocrisy and greed for wealth destroy the soul and harm the health.
While nations starve and factions war, this bitter wrath will evermore
Stain the hearts of those who follow, render offspring weak and hollow;
Except that men of moral heart, in leadership, shall play their part.

Grief, depression, heartache, tears, the harvest of two thousand years;
This legacy was made by choice of those who would ignore the voice . . .
Of reason, knowledge and goodwill, of One whose power is greater still
Than any known to you or I – the choice is yours . . . to live or die."

With this, the impulse engines fired, the ghostly figure then retired.
On farewell gesture of his hand, applause resounded through the land.
Resplendent was her take-off power, kaleidoscopic laser shower,
Majestic thus, her parting flight, in blink of eye was gone from sight.

The President, a fluent man, and wise in things semantic
Unfazed by gross hysteria of paparazzi frantic,
When asked for his reaction to this stranger from the sky,
In pensive tone, with measured calm, he offered his reply.

"Let history mark this great event a turning point in man's intent.
For Truth alone shall render whole the ethos of the human soul.
The laws of which our comrade spoke, and his request that we invoke
Their timeless gift, once carved in stone, confirms that
   . . . we are not alone!"

A poem for the Millennium.

THE CONFINES OF THE MIND

What predatory forces find
The fissured confines of the mind!
Where gnarled hobgoblin's sharpened pick
With sins long past, does conscience prick.

In inglenooks with balustrades
Where ghosts sip tainted lemonades;
With poisoned darts they irk and needle,
Spook and startle, twist and wheedle.

Oh! How those visions, dark and ghoulish
Haunt the wakes of actions foolish.
Wherein black spectres of regret
In wraith-like form, their vengeance get.

They feed on notions of the lustful
Drink betrayal's wine distrustful,
Yet unassuaged, their appetites
Will prey in dark, tormenting nights.

For none escape their gruesome hand;
Reality's no perfect land.
Its battleground, in truth must lie
In human mind . . . not earth or sky.

How certain he must end in tears
Who takes no counsel of the years;
Nor heeds the words of sages past
Who fathomed how man's die was cast.

So bitter come the tempter's thanks
For those who dwell within his ranks
In selfish quest, for their tomorrow
Comes in darkness . . . draped with sorrow.

A POET'S HEART

A poet's heart's an endless thing,
Ubiquitous, encompassing.
It knows no bound nor borderline,
Or darkness where it may not shine.

A poet's heart's a joyful thing,
It likes to laugh, and loves to sing.
It lifts the spirit, holds it high,
Then dances like a firefly.

A poet's heart's a fragile thing,
As brittle as a monarch's wing.
That flutters on a breath of air,
The secrets of its soul to bare.

A poet's heart's a vicious thing,
Its bite is like a hornet's sting.
For it will strike just as and when
It feels the censure of its pen.

A poet's heart's a caring thing,
Both empathy and hope to bring.
A sunbeam's touch it can impart
To mollify the saddened heart.

A poet's heart's a timeless thing,
Whose ancient bell sustains its ring.
That through the years, it may adorn
Those generations yet unborn.

HUMOUR

CHEERS!

This poetry writing's not always a doddle
One moment there's motive, the next there is soddle.
I sit at my keyboard and tinker all day
Then if nothing comes right, I just give it away!

I use all the letters, and some of the fun-keys;
If that doesn't work, well, I don't give a monkey's.
Sometimes it will gel, it's a matter of luck;
That some verses will sing, and some others will suck!

No, it's not really true, I'm just having a laugh,
As I often compose all my lines in the bath;
Then rush to my desk whilst they're fresh in my mind
With a shower of bathwater dripping behind!

New Zealand's hot evenings are splendid for writing
Cicadas keep singing, and mozzies keep biting.
Cold Lion Red's sweet, so I'll reach for a bottle;
Few words come at first, but then surely a lot'll!

IN PRAISE OF OLDER WOMEN

Beset me not with Baywatch girls
Whose haughty looks and Pantene curls
May cause my weary head to rest
Upon a cool synthetic breast!

But speak to me of angels eyes,
Of silken skin and slender thighs;
Where grace, fine honed by poise demure
Reflects her charms in haute couture.

Wherein the mellow, genteel mind
Brooks elegance of style refined;
Endearing charm so warmly granting
Charismatic smile enchanting.

So let the wanton eye perceive
The full bikini's sway and heave.
Much better far a sporty, naughty
Cultured lady . . . over forty!

SOON PARTED

You jingle, you jangle, on paper you're sweet
Your touch in my wallet is pleasing and neat.
But it doesn't last long, it happens a lot
One moment you're there, and the next you are not.

I can't help myself, if a bargain I see
Or if I buy one I will get one for free.
Just one small deposit and nothing to pay . . .
Six months down the track I am ruing the day!

The ad men are ruthless, they play on my faults
They think there's no end to the gold in my vaults.
"Just buy now and save!" they continually harp
They're all out to get me – and, bugger, they're sharp!

I go to the doctor – I've broken my arm
My pain doesn't faze the receptionist's charm
"I really don't care if you've broken your neck . . .
Now will it be EFTPOS, or cash . . . or by cheque?"

I love you, I hate you, temptation fantastic;
In form electronic on card made of plastic.
Seducer of men since time long before Caesar
Disguised now as Mastercard, Amex or Visa.

– Soon Parted –

But hard cash is favourite, I find that, with credit,
My statement depresses me when I have read it.
We writers earn little, as well we all know
A publisher's life seems the best way to go!

I've not seen a poor one, alone on the street,
They seem to have plenty to drink and to eat.
That which they produce fills their coffers and shelves
Yet little of it have they written themselves!

Beset by a whim, I consulted my wife;
Sure, who but a fool goes soliciting strife?
"All poets are foolish" – I grin with a sigh . . .
"Not all fools are poets" then dawns my reply!

BED OF EDELWEISS

She's a fashion super-model, she's the talk of every town;
She can cut it in a swimsuit or a slinky velvet gown.
She may tantalize with that walk which she learned upon the catwalk
But beneath the glitz and fat talk, somewhere lies a scornful frown.

Let other poets write of her, for she will make her mark
On those who see so fine a tree, but not beyond its bark.
Resplendent though at first she seems, in singlet and designer jeans
She's not the best, by any means, yet all men will remark . . .

They'll speak, perhaps, of how she walks, or how she wears her hair
Or of how that faded denim shows a trace of underwear.
Just a teasing little wave'll show a ruby studded navel
And bewitch them so they rave all 'bout her shapely derriere.

Let other poets write of her, then let them still repose
She is nothing but a daisy to the beauty of my rose;
Such charismatic gracefulness! Those smiling eyes! I must confess
I'd give my life, her soul to bless, were I the one she chose.

When she whispers to me . . . nice! I am melted in a trice
Its as though I am reclining on a bed of Edelweiss.
She has style, charm and taste . . . *and* a supermodels waist
Ah! . . . and just a splash of sweet Panache . . . and I'm in paradise!

Ah! It softens and endears, does the beauty of the years
And it's often born of matters torn by heartache and by tears.
Let the supermodels flouncing keep a-swaying and a-bouncing
I will settle for the mettle of the one who soothes my fears.

FAITH

THE DOVE

Mute hangs the winter's icy chill
Grey morning mist lies bleak and still;
And silence, like a spectre, reigns;
Save footfalls, where the snow remains.

No breath of wind greets frosted bough
Suspended, it is ghost-like now.
Ethereal, its woody fingers
Rake, but still the cold fog lingers.

Bereft of reason, paused in time,
The mourners in their grief combine,
As callous clouds of anguish smother
Family and weeping mother.

And none will deign to hide or mask it,
As bearers bring the tiny casket
White, wreathed, adorned with Cross of gold,
It nestles in their careful hold.

As all in sombre bonding stand,
The scene knows neither time nor land.
And all here present feel its breath;
Its iceberg touch . . . its kiss of death.

Its tendrils, dark and sinister
Encompass all . . . the minister
Takes solace in a silent prayer,
And begs the Lord his burden share.

Thus all in sorrow stand around
The waiting void of new-dug ground
Its earthy walls . . . its cold embrace
A desolate, unfeeling place.

A dozen faces, gaunt and pale
Give echo to the mother's wail;
For, if the choice were theirs to make,
Each one, the child's place would take.

Remote, the numbing second thrives,
The little coffin then arrives;
Such hanging pall of grim despair
Defies the human soul to bear . . .

A mother's pain, that tears apart
The very sinews of her heart
Which shrieks the plaintive, searing cry
"What have I done? – for God's sake WHY?"

So sudden – in her darkest hour
A vision blossoms like a flower!
A portal dark, with light is gifted.
A Damoclean sword is lifted.

She sees green hills with sparkling waters
And countless million sons and daughters.
Creeds and colours of all ages . . .
The book of life's unopened pages.

The partly written page, unfinished,
The postponed parchment, undiminished.
And those for whom all teardrops fall . . .
The ones which have no words at all.

There's no disease, no lies, no hate,
For these remain at Heaven's gate;
They know no pain, they voice no cries,
A love-light shines within their eyes.

She's drawn towards a quiet brook
A white-robed form with shepherd's crook.
His gentle manner strong, yet mild,
And, in his arms, her little child.

In that brief instant, time was stilled;
Her heart with warm contentment filled.
And, in His light, she found the power
That e'er sustains the unknown hour.

Reality again returns,
Though in her heart the vision burns.
Its everlasting, hallowed flame
Restores and dignifies again.

With tear-filled eyes, and hands that shook,
The Vicar gently closed the Book.
From his right hand, a dusty curtain
Falls, in hope that's sure and certain.

Then radiant breaks the morning sun;
The vanquished mist flees at a run.
As silver spangled jeweled beams
In dancing yellows, golds and creams . . .

Shine warmly on the little grave,
The snow, its thawed surrender gave
In melting yield, its remnants grooming
Crocus flower and snowdrop blooming.

She wonders if it's all a dream . . .
The Shepherd's crook . . . the shining stream?
Whose attestation brooks denial
Within the nightmares of her trial.

Her ears discern a call . . . a sound!
Her gaze, on rising from the ground,
Beholds, poised on a limb above . . .
. . . A solitary snow-white dove.

Her wings unfold, with grace she glides,
Then o'er the little grave presides;
Divine, her presence signifies
This child in full salvation lies.

In glorious farewell, she flies
To silver sun and sapphire skies.
Redemption's herald, winged and white;
The candle . . . in a mother's night.

"In pastures green; he leadeth me
. . . the quiet waters by." Psalm 23.

THE GARDEN OF YOUR HEART

Oh, mystery of life! You ever deepen with the rolling years;
Your vast arrayed enigmas are as endless as man's tears
Shed for his own kind, that not one soul of millions passed
Had found the key that would unlock the secret spell you cast.

Our scientists, philosophers, astronomers and kings
All strive to find the reasons for man's endless sufferings;
Whilst writers, poets, lyricists combine to paint the scene
The hunger and the wars go on, abhorrent and obscene.

Will man discover answers that will right the human race
In faint, ethereal signals beaming down from outer space?
And will those answers terminate the warlord's bloody lust;
Or feed the child dying in Sudan's hot sun-baked dust?

Incessant drive to interfere with nature's manufacture
To feed the earth with chemicals and change genetic structure
Beware! The cold, grey fingers rise – of sickness and fatigue;
The haunting, spectral legacies of the Corporates and their greed.

Consider – interstellar quest is fraught with human error
Better far, to look within to end this reign of terror;
To contemplate, and understand the Great Designer's plan
And see that what is needed is to change the heart of man.

When the forces of the darkness, and the forces of the Light
Clash daily in your conscience, urging sanity to flight;
When the claws of doubt are tearing at the fabric of your soul
And deny you right of access in the pursuit of your goal;

Then turn your searchlight inwards to the core of your foundation
Rekindle there the fire of Life, and banish condemnation
Re-plant the seeds of right and truth in the garden of your heart;
For never seed has starved nor died where love has played its part.

THE SILENT PREACHER

How still the night air – cool and clean
With city lights from hilltop seen.
Beneath the heavens, starred and bright
With arms outstretched into the night . . .

Behold! – the silent preacher stands
His branches like so many hands
That reach out to a moonlit sky
To praise her silver lullaby.

He stands in peaceful homage – yet
Majestically, his silhouette
Adorns the great celestial charms . . .
And stars seem drawn toward his arms.

His countless fronds, like fingers, mark
A million courses through the dark
As if to signify the maze
A man must face throughout his days.

Then – look beyond his outward show
And see what saints and angels know;
His mighty trunk, in armour cased
Is on a strong foundation based.

His heartline runs both straight and true
Is such a message there for you?
He speaks no words, yet with this sign
The Lord's hand blessed . . . the Norfolk Pine.

THE LILY

Oh, elegant flower, how noble you tower
Your poise and your grace you display;
To catch by and by the beholder's eye
Reflecting the new light of day.

Your bloom tells the story of nature's full glory
The hand that designed you could only be Truth;
For only the power that conceived the first hour
Could so gift you with eternal youth.

There is none can compare with your beauty so rare
With your ball gown so verdant and fine;
Your complexion of white puts all darkness to flight;
Your creation a matter divine.

Your symmetry sings and your petals are wings
Lifting your gaze to the skies;
Caressed by the breeze, you acknowledge the trees
As they whisper enchanted replies.

Whilst the dewdrops adorn your perfection of form
And you bask in your spotlight of gold;
I reflect on the pleasure you give beyond measure
To those with the time to behold.

– The Lily –

As I ponder the mystery of your ancestral history
I stand humbled by feelings sublime;
You have changed not in time, since the Genesis line
Was first drawn on the vast sands of time.

Your magic is told in great stories of old
In manifold mention you feature;
But you reached highest glory in scriptural story
Crowned queen above all by the Teacher.

*"For I say unto you that even Solomon in all his glory
is not arrayed like one of these." Luke 12 v27.*

THE CACTUS

I have a little cactus
It was given as a gift
And every time I look at it
It makes my spirit lift.

Upon its verdant canopy
Three little flowers bloom
Like candles on a birthday cake
Or torches in the gloom.

I cannot touch their glory
It's protected well, you see
But I will tell the story
Of the way that they touch me.

The gift of their salvation
Is a sharp and spiny shield
Such foreboding castigation
Once did Roman soldiers wield.

A cruelly woven crown of thorns
Once placed upon a head
Considered mortal, now adorns
A diadem instead.

– The Cactus –

They couldn't mask His power
And they couldn't break His will
In crimson shower of cactus flower
His splendour shines through still.

In growing, and in casting
Thorns will fade in time . . . and go
But in beauty everlasting
Shall remain what lies below.

In the hand of friendship, granting
This, and far more do I see
In the eyes of the enchanting
Love, who gave this flower to me.

CONFLICT

THE FLAG

Come, all who rise to greet each dawn in disaffected manner,
Yet daily walk in favour born of freedom's sovereign banner;
Then ponder well your shield of Union flag and Southern Cross,
And edge in gilt the men who built her mast of tragic loss.

See her ride the wind with pride! She draws her halyards tauter,
In proud salute to those who bore her far across the water.
Her tribute to her sons and daughters, conscious of her price.
And those she lost, who paid her cost in blood . . . and sacrifice.

Beneath the verdant canopies of Asia's long campaign
The Kiwi footprint once was found where now it walks again.
Not river's flow nor sunset's glow its memory could erase
For one, its image long will carry, 'til his final days.

Just one more Kiwi soldier with his sworn allegiance true
To banner starred and spangled bright on sea of royal blue.
In dire threat from forces dark and of his own perdition,
The politicians backed his cause – with verbal ammunition.

As from their lofty corridors of self-perceived noblesse,
They gambled with the lives of men in Asia's game of chess.
That you and I should live the joy of countless peaceful dawns,
Is not our debt to knights or kings, but courage of the pawns.

Ah, – courage? Yes, they talk of her, in eloquent oration.
Such plausible magniloquence concerning State and Nation.
Yet were they present with him in that bloodstained Asian river
With bayonet fixed, emotions mixed, and stomach churning quiver?

Alas – not so, it seems as though the protocols of war
Dictate that they be far away upon a leeward shore;
Too far to see the jungle vast, nor feel its stifling heat;
Or hear the sub-machine gun blast its grim staccato beat.

As on that fateful day, patrolling waist deep in the slime,
Reality became his nightmare in a trice of time;
That fiery flash of ambush scattered all upon the scene
And stilled the heart of his best friend, who was a Royal Marine.

Who would no more the trial endure of suppurating sore,
The gauntlet of malaria, and leeches by the score,
Nor threat of rodent's poisoned bite, nor sting of eyes infected;
He'd done his job, for them, for us, his duty as directed.

Now if the orators perchance to knock on Heaven's door,
God grant it may be opened by a child of East Timor.
In battle past, the die was cast, but democratic right
Died in procrastination's bloody never-ending night.

And so the child may lead them where the mists of time enshroud
A land where all men dwell in peace below a long white cloud.
Wherein her heroes gather still, in hallowed dawn parade.
They wonder sometimes . . . "Is it worth the sacrifice we made?"

Behold these men assembled here beneath the Standard's mast.
Beside each one, a vacant place, without a shadow cast.
Where souls of comrades lost abide, by human eye unseen;
One Kiwi, one Australian . . . and . . . a British Royal Marine.

THE FINAL CALL

They'd considered him a hero in the place where he was born,
In that town beneath the mountains, near the sea.
He had fought in places far away, by savage conflict torn,
With the hope he might help others to be free.

He had seen the wrath of nature, its ferocity withstood;
And he'd witnessed hate and bigotry and lies;
But he'd done his duty proudly, in the quest for common good
In his land, and under distant, lonely skies.

But then times must change, and friendships fade, and life itself conclude,
Then his final homeward pilgrimage began.
Where the memories of the few who loved him changed
    with time renewed,
And his ashes claimed the ground where once he ran.

He had made that greatest sacrifice . . . is it to be in vain?
Shall his heirs not see the dawn of freedom's light?
And how shall we convince ourselves he perished without pain,
In the blistered heart of conflict's endless night?

It seems to make it bearable, convincing, though untrue
That his deeds would teach us lessons that endure.
But in sweet and blissful ignorance the sins of man accrue.
Still the consequence of violence is sure.

Yet it was for him, the final call, he'd not be asked again
To face the awful ravages of war.
To take up arms, to kill and die, for bloody tyrants' gain
Thus feed their lustful appetites for more.

Now his brothers, sons and daughters too, march past in jungle greens,
Undaunted as they follow in his tracks.
Too soon their pride and honour will give way to shattered dreams
As their grand illusions wane like molten wax.

So they depart for distant shores, where moguls rest at leisure,
To write their closing epitaphs in blood,
They'll pay the price in life and limb, as warlords hoard their treasure.
Yet scarce restrain this dark, foreboding flood.

Is this to be our destiny for countless years to come,
That the white dove from her chosen path transgress?
Must freedom be subverted by the missile and the gun
Hot condiments of war – such bitterness!

Then will all his years of tribulation yield for us no gain?
Cruel harvest makes the fodder of the rich.
Shall his kinfolk not abide in peace, bereft of guilt and pain?
Not forgotten in a bloody roadside ditch.

Of countless number passed before, he's surely not the last;
Though honest men hold dear his proclamations.
His hero's badge lies tarnished in the mists of ages past
While the cursed hand of death still haunts our nations.

He'd done his best, but in the grip of failure's icy claw
Grows stronger still the lust to kill and maim.
He gave his all to edify, to bring an end to war;
Yet human folly lingers . . . just the same.

For me, for you, no greater love could this man ever show
Than the forfeit of his own life for his friend.
His hero's soul now rests fulfilled – 'twas written long ago
Whilst love has life, she'll triumph . . . in the end.

Co-authored with Emanuel Seafont.

LOVE

THIS CATHEDRAL

I want you to be happy, but I seem to make you cry,
For a little teardrop glistens in the corner of your eye.
In the softness of its waters I see how you truly feel,
As in the corner of your heart, I humbly bow . . . and kneel.

I am silent, I am lowly, I am totally in awe
I am witnessing a miracle I've never seen before.
And here, within this hallowed place, my eyes begin to chart
The power and the splendour of a Christian woman's heart.

I can see the damaged tissue that was once so scarred and bruised
Where the daggers of betrayal left you bleeding and abused.
Where the mirrors of your infancy, once burnished bright as gold
Lay tarnished with the images of broken dreams of old.

I can see the mighty firestones where the flames of childbirth blazed
And the plaques of dedication, for the years when they were raised.
I can see the shield of valour, for your courage, and your stand
In the face of their adversity . . . and death's precocious hand.

There's a limpid pool of crystal where your wishing coins were cast
There is one for every sentimental moment of your past.
They are made of gold and silver, but of copper there are some
With gentlest kiss, I make a wish . . . for all that's yet to come.

There's the haunting, muffled drumbeat of your pulsing heart so dear
It is calling to its soul mate . . . it is music to my ear.
There's a glowing warmth surrounding me, it speaks of truth above
Of beauty, art and poetry, and soft eternal love.

Rising upward, as a mountain, is your solid Rock of faith
It is shining opalescent like a gleaming silver wraith.
And it carries every burden, every sorrow, seen or heard
For on its face is carved the promise of the living Word.

Then it dawns upon me slowly, and it makes me shudder so
For I recognize the beauty of this iridescent glow!
I have seen it in your laughter, I have felt it through your sighs,
It's the heart of your foundation . . . and it's right there . . . in your eyes!

I have seen a thousand sunsets and their dappled, painted skies
In the dawn I've seen the colours of the pheasant on the rise.
Though I've seen the summer's glory in the flowers and the trees;
Your eyes exceed by far indeed the total sum of these.

I am deeply moved and humbled by my presence in this place
Just to know you, just to love you, just to look upon your face.
And I'd like to make my home here, that we never more shall part.
In this glorious cathedral . . . that is called your woman's heart.

REFLECTIONS OF YOUR HEART

Fonder grows the love that glows in absence' lonely light,
I count the days 'til you will rest safe in my arms at night;
In times as these, when life decrees that we must be apart
I glimpse, in nature's glory, true reflections of your heart.

As summer's evening falls, and the soft horizon calls
The golden sun to rest within her endless wings of blue,
Her burning heart will sleep beneath the nightfall's starry keep;
Across the ocean deep, she heralds twilight's purple hue.

The sun-kissed breeze so calming as it brushes 'gainst my cheek;
The jewel-spangled beams that play their games of hide and seek;
Remind me of your sweet caress, and strolls along the sand,
The tender warmth of your soft lips, the touch of your dear hand.

The last rays kiss the leaves that shimmer in the trees so tall,
As dappled shadows dance around your picture on the wall;
The sweet songbird, she calls to me, her evening hymn to share,
Then father time begins to chime his haunting mellow air.

As echoes of the night-time steal away the seagull's cries;
The rolling song of lapping surf is hushed by mist that lies
In valleys gowned with heather fading down to sandy shores;
These whispers of the evening are forever mine and yours.

Though all these years has nature shed her colours o'er the scene,
A home without a heart is like a girl without a dream;
When you alone safe home return, and cradle in my arms,
Our souls shall rest in true love blessed with nature's tranquil charms.

MORNING LOVE

The rising light of summer's dawn
That twinkles bright through curtains drawn
And shimmers on her sleeping form
To wrap her in a silver storm.

Dancing sunbeams mystic cluster
Gilding her with golden lustre.
Watch and comfort, love and trust her
Touch her like a feather duster.

Whispers . . . like a poet writing
Dreams of some euphoric sighting.
Eyes awaken . . . lips alighting
Softly touching . . . and delighting.

Burnished glow of arms entwining
Keeps the love-light ever shining
In the dawn's soft light reclining.
Blissful, total, sweet resigning.

IN YOUR EYES

Rising dawn
New-born fawn
Misty softness of the morn.
Spangled bright
Deep insight
Yields the secrets of the night.

Morning tea
You and me
Mirrors of the sparkling sea.
Crystal sheen
Glycerine
Soothing, gentle and serene.

Afternoon
Shades of June
Brighter than the harvest moon.
Born anew
Honey-dew
Shimmers in a pastel hue.

Eventide
Deep inside
All the sorrows that you hide.
Feel the pain
Start again
Melting almond in the rain.

– In Your Eyes –

Come the night
Candle light
Ice on fire, translucent . . . bright.
Opalescent
Incandescent
Shines a love-light, iridescent.

Pools of fire
Beam desire
Burning upward, ever higher.
Touch and kiss
Perfect bliss
In your eyes . . . such love . . . as this.

STORM OF PASSION

A vivid flash of light igniting sapphire studded sky;
The rolling thunder growling, like a tiger in full cry.
The fury of a million raindrops, pounding overhead.
All make us truly thankful for the comfort of our bed.

Now the tempest gathers impulse as the night is closing in;
Like the power of my heartbeat 'gainst the softness of your skin.
And your fingers running gently through my golden strands of hair
Spur the driving force of nature as she rises to prepare . . .

The crescendo of the heavens, in a blinding cannonade
Like a thousand philharmonics, as a symphony is played.
There is lightning for the cymbals, there is thunder for the drums
And the raindrops are percussion, and the wind, euphoniums.

Soon our lips are touching softly, and our bodies are as one
And I hold you to me gently, like its only just begun.
I am tracing all the contours of your valleys and your peaks
As we tremble with sensations . . . such that neither of us speaks.

Now the pelting rain is driving and the storm is full-on pitch
Is the window frame vibrating? Or the glass? I can't tell which.
She is towering in her majesty, impassioned in her flight
As her overtures pay homage to the glory of this night.

We are moving to her rhythm, to the beating of her heart
She is taking us to paradise with all she can impart.
We are sailing on her echoes, in a chariot of fire
Through a cauldron of emotion in a furnace of desire.

We are lost in this kaleidoscope of jewel-tinted whorls
There is fire in the deepness of our honey-moistened curls.
Sweet oblivion is total, not a trace of mortal time,
Just a love-light in our passion, so ethereal . . . sublime.

In the morning comes the silence, with the ruddy glow of dawn,
For her parting has bequeathed to us the beauty of this morn.
And your eyes possess her lustre, for they sparkle clear and bright
Like the opalescent colours . . . of the tempest of the night.

MY BUTTERFLY

Standing at my window, with the evening sun above,
I could feel you touch my heartbeat with your special kind of love.
And I let its warmth surround me, and the glow within your shield;
Not a sunset, nor a rosebud, or a mother's touch could yield.

I watched a passing Monarch, on the summer breeze she flew,
And her soft, enchanting loveliness reminded me of you.
Then I noticed something special, and it touched me to the core
It was more than just her beauty . . . 'twas the burden that she bore.

'Neath her wings of flaming orange, she was carrying within
Her tiny feet . . . a dying member of her kith and kin.
Though its wings were torn and tattered, and its little heart forlorn
There'd be power in the healing of the dewy mists of morn.

Once before, I've seen such courage, and I knew this was a sign
In the glory of that butterfly, I felt your hand in mine.
And the life she gave her soul mate, through her brave heart,
    strong and free
It was mirrored in the echoes of the love you've shown to me.

When my heart was sad and heavy, and my wings were torn and frayed
You lifted up my life again, we laughed . . . and then we prayed.
The Lord rejoiced to hear your voice, He knew what I had seen
You'll always be my butterfly . . . my Monarch . . . and my Queen.

THE DEWDROP AND THE ROSE

Love is in the morning dewdrop that enfolds his moist embrace
'Round the newly dawning rosebud as she turns her pastel face
To the glory of the sunrise . . . then she bids her last goodbyes
To the night-time's fading shadows . . . and the splendour of her skies.

In the gleaming mellow sauna of the slowly rising mist
Comes a haunting recollection of the lips that once I kissed
Now their velvet charms entrance me . . . and for moments they abide
Like fairy seeds of dandelion upon a fairground ride.

As the rosebud gently opens and the dewdrop falls away
With his dying remnants fading in the newborn warmth of day
Glowing petals bloom and shimmer with a beauty rich and rare
And a radiance that, but for love, could not have lingered there.

Somewhere deep within the darkness, in the confines of the night
Love had cast its jeweled sequins in the silver moon's soft light.
There is power in the healing whose caress all life sustains
He may vanish with the sunlight, but his legacy remains.

He came not with cries of passion, nor with promises of power
But with grace, in love abiding through the silence of the hour.
In her dreams and smiles and sorrows, still his spirit shall remain
As it was from the beginning . . . and will surely be again.

JUST LIKE A KING

I pour another coffee, and I light a cigarette
I have no heart for stereo, T.V. or Internet.
The telephone is silent, but I pray that you will ring
For I long to feel the happiness that only you can bring.

There is emptiness without you, for you are my closest friend
And the comfort of your presence is a thing I miss no end.
It's a sharing, it's a calmness, it's a privilege and pleasure
And, to me, it is a priceless thing, impossible to measure.

Now my heart is aching sorely, for the time is ticking by
And my prowess as a poet is reducing to a sigh.
Yet, there is a consolation that our friendship does allow
For I know that, somewhere in the dark, you're thinking of me now.

And once again, my spirit lifts, I think of sunny days . . .
A dreamy walk upon a hill that overlooks the bays.
Where, tenderly, you took my hand, you did not move away,
And for me, those precious moments were like Heaven for a day.

You made me feel just like a King, but riches can't compare
With the way your eyes were smiling as the wind blew through your hair.
I'll remember it forever, until all my days are done.
The blessed memory of my day beside you . . . in the sun.

Someday, I hope to hold you, and again rebuild your trust
And help to heal those scars of lies, deception . . . and of lust
So, for what I'm worth, I'm here on earth . . . and God is there above you.
By His great power such blessings shower – how very much I love you!

I know I'm not the first to say such tender words to you
And how their shattered dreams have made you feel forsaken, too.
For, in all my life, I've known the pain of broken dreams as well
They can take a life of happiness, and make it bloody hell.

Such destiny could only come from God's Almighty hands
That brought us both together from our distant native lands,
Every night I kneel and thank Him for His mercy from above
And for all I've ever wanted . . . in the woman that I love.

THE EAGLE

I took my thoughts and gave them to the eagle
She soared into a sky of pale blue;
From sun kissed wings, and talons bright as silver,
She cast them to the wind in search of you.

Then thunderclouds caressed them into raindrops,
That fell, and sparkled softly, like champagne;
So you would know when I was thinking of you,
My thoughts, my tears, would touch you in the rain.

A kind thought, like a smile, is given freely,
And springs from somewhere deep within the soul;
Your thoughts, to me, are more than gold and silver,
They give me hope, and strength, and make me whole.

For kindred spirits, distance has no story,
And time can do no damage to their cause;
From earth's first dawn until its dying glory,
Their hopes and dreams entwine, as mine and yours.

GENTLE POET

Gentle poet, breathe on me,
That I may your soul-mate be.
Let me reach inside your heart,
As you did right from the start.

Tell me how you truly feel.
In your spirit, let me kneel.
Hold my hand and let me share
All the treasure buried there.

Let the mortal spark rekindle,
Nevermore to ebb . . . or dwindle.
Make its bright flames flare and dart
In the fireplace of my heart.

Etch your words upon my soul
Seared in fire of burning coal
Walk me to my journey's end
Gentle poet . . . my best friend.

PRICELESS

I could feel my teardrops falling, and so many had I shed
They were running like a streamlet flowing down upon my bed
As they scorched apart my burning heart, meandering to seek
The oasis of our friendship, where the strong supports the weak.

I was crying in a darkness, I was looking for a light
When I heard your gentle whisper asking if I was all right.
Then the stream became a deluge, and before the hour was through
I had shared the flowing passions of my aching soul with you.

Though my tears were as a baby, 'twas your love that saw me through
As you softly reassured me – and you understood me, too.
Like a rock, you gave me shelter, as you promised you'd be there
For me always – even in my darkest valley of despair.

Like a rock, no, not just any, but a stone of brightest hue
Yet, no diamond, ever priceless, is worth half as much as you.
Now another is restraining you, but time has come to pass
And, where once he loved this diamond, now he just sees only glass.

Now my tears return in number, and my breaking heart, he weeps
For this diamond must be cherished, loved and cuddled up for keeps
She is precious, she is beautiful, her sparkle only part
Of her loveliness, and I know this – for I have seen her heart.

Long ago, there was betrayal, she was sold as Judas did
With a kiss that was as meaningless – and she was lost amid
All her anguish and her suffering, so sorely did she pine
Yet throughout the years, and all her tears, she's never lost her shine.

You're a gem beyond description, brighter far than any star,
And I love you for the essence of the woman that you are.
The Lord Himself has blessed you – and I know . . . I've seen His mark
Within the eyes of my true love – my diamond in the dark.

THE LAST PRAYER

The mighty waves engulf me, they are driving from the West,
Like a thundering leviathan, ice-cold from trough to crest.
A howling savage haunts me, and he cuts me like a knife;
It's the demon wind of satan . . . on the ocean of my life.

Beyond the water's roaring, I can hear the seabird's cry
High above the seething rollers, where the foaming horses fly.
With the salted echoes rising 'gainst the current's tidal race
I'm confronting my mortality . . . it stares me in the face.

How those breakers rise in majesty, and run before the storm!
With agate-like lucidity in ever changing form.
Their anger is an entity, it's like a thing possessed
That knows no bounds of time or space, nor any place to rest.

Now their fury is upon me – a tsunami bearing down
In a massive wall of water, with its white-topped speckled crown.
And its undertow is taking me to where there's no return
I shall drown without forgiveness . . . then I'll go to hell . . . and burn.

Then I see her . . . like a vision, as my lifetime flashes by
To the keening of the devil's breath . . . his caustic lullaby.
In her eyes, there was forgiveness, there was Heaven in her smile,
She had given me completeness . . . she had made it all worthwhile.

The happiness she gave to me, it's with me at the end
Though I've no more part of her life, she's forever my best friend.
There's her whisper . . . in my last prayer . . . e'er my
    beating heart shall sleep;
Jesus . . . save me! . . . from the ever pounding forces of the deep.

WITHOUT YOU

The mountainside is steeper now, without your guiding hand
The ocean cold and deeper now, with no warmth in the sand.
The grass is dry and barren since you went upon your way,
I thought it would be fleeting, but it happens every day.

I'm looking for the words to tell you what you mean to me.
I want them to be special, as that's what you've come to be.
It wasn't meant to happen but the hand of fortune plays
The secret cards of destiny in many different ways.

There are times when I am lonely, and I whisper out your name.
It seems to help me somehow, but I miss you just the same.
The songbird greets the evening, and the sunset marks the hour.
I see your looks reflected in the petals of a flower.

I recall the morning dewdrop springing sweetly from the rose
And the calling of the songthrush as she wakes from her repose.
But their elegance is wanting, and their splendour has no cheer
Like the healing in your fingers, or your whisper in my ear.

As the twilight falls around me, and I pray a silent prayer,
I ask the Lord to watch you, and to take you in His care.
As the stars begin to twinkle, and the moon begins to rise,
I have seen a rarer beauty in the colours of your eyes.

Now the night is closing faster and my spirit's getting low;
I ponder one last vision of the you I've come to know.
It's a comfort, it's a longing, and it fills my aching heart
Bitter-sweet my contemplation of the days we've been apart.

Us . . . Being Us

We both love hanging baskets
And we both love heart-to-hearts.
We both love mochaccinos
And we both love strawberry tarts.

We both love parks and gardens
And we both love dreamy walks.
We both love apple donuts
And we both love cosy talks.

We both love writing poems
And we both love singing songs.
We both love little keepsakes
And we both love righting wrongs.

We both love lakes and forests
And we both love flowers and trees.
We both love dawns and sunsets
And we both love summer breeze.

We both love chocolate ice-cream
And we both love shopping trips.
We both love climbing mountains
And we both love sailing ships.

But one thing we like best of all
It's how its come to be . . .

That I love loving you
As much as you love loving me.

ABOUT THE AUTHOR

ROD WALFORD

I was born in Shoreham, Sussex, England in 1950. At the age of eight, I went to the British Seamens' Boys' Home at Brixham in South Devon, where I remained until I left school in 1966. The home, famous throughout Devon, was originally founded as a haven for orphaned sons of British sailors. In the early fifties, a decision was taken to accept boys from single parent circumstances, as there were fewer orphans needing care. Life at the home was conducted under British Royal Navy protocol, and boys were groomed for future service at sea. However, a career in the Royal Navy was by no means compulsory, and there was total freedom to follow a career of choice.

Discipline was strictly enforced, and participation in Home's drum and bugle band was mandatory. I learned to play the bugle soon after joining, and by the time I had reached the age of fifteen, I had attained the position of lead bugler. This carried the prestige of a silver bugle and shoulder sash. Some of my most abiding memories stem from visiting various Churches on Remembrance Day to play the "Last Post" and "Reveille." The band would also perform at a variety of soccer matches, fetes, carnivals and garden parties, in addition to our regular Sunday morning church parade.

At the age of eleven, I was fortunate enough to gain admission to Homelands Technical High School in nearby Torquay. English was the subject that I enjoyed the most, and I will always be grateful to have been tutored by some very dedicated teachers during my five years at Homelands.

During my years at the Home, I developed a passion for engines. The Home had two motor-boats and a diesel engine used to pump seawater to fill the swimming pool. I was involved in helping to maintain all of these. I was averse to the coarse blue serge material of the Royal Navy uniform and found it very uncomfortable to wear, particularly when wet. Thus I resolved to follow a civilian career and when I left Brixham at the age of sixteen, I trained to become a diesel engine fuel injection specialist.

I had a spell in the British Army, followed by complete break from my trade when, in 1978, I spent thirteen years in the field of water supply and treatment. I emigrated to New Zealand in 1991, once again returning to the fuel injection trade.

I have an intense dislike of all cruelty, especially to children and animals, and become dismayed by man's ever increasing inhumanity to his fellow man, as depicted daily on television news. I enjoy most sports, motorsport in particular, and my other hobbies include playing chess, listening to music and writing poetry.

I feel that poetry is a unique way of communicating with people of like-minded spirit. It is an opportunity for expression of thought and feeling within the framework of the writer's own choosing. It allows the reader freedom to empathize or criticize, in much the same way as an art lover would study an artist's canvas. In many ways, I think a poem is similar to a painting. Unlike a novel, it usually takes only minutes to read, yet the impressions conveyed can linger in the memory like a vision.

Over the years, I have learned many lessons the hard way. Through this has come a greater understanding of what are commonly referred to as old-fashioned moral values; the values of trust, loyalty, true friendship and, above all, love. I believe this to be the greatest of all emotions, and I have tried to reflect its power in much of my poetry.

Through the medium of poetry, I have made many loyal friends. Nowhere more so than in my own local writers' group. To have shared in their fellowship has been a blessing of inestimable worth. Here, I have seen a true reflection of all these values.

My favourite classic poets are Lord Byron and Rudyard Kipling. Kipling's poem "If" says it all for me. I constantly refer to it, either for inspiration or in times of hardship. Byron's mastery of language also inspires me when I am searching for a semantic illustration.

INDEX

INDEX